Affirmations for Purposeful Living

Manifesting Health, Wholeness and Joy

Michèle Marie Gervais

Affirmations for Purposeful Living
Copyright © 2018 by Michele Marie Gervais

Photo Credit: Janis Dow Heart First Photography
Editor: Dixie Dash

Cover Photo: Bee with Sunflower

The sunflower represents the unique sun radiant individuality
of the I AM Presence. The beautiful spark of light found
within each Being. It is a symbolic expression of vitality
drawn from the Sun Source of life to fuel the flowering of one's
gifts, realizing potential. The bee is about Creation and the
Honey of Life. The activity of the bee is purposeful, it assists
flowers and fruits to blossom and reach potential. The bee is
a reminder to look into our own activity and to ask ourselves
two important questions: "Are my actions purposeful,
creating a meaningful life?" and "Am I taking the time to
enjoy the fruits of my labour, basking in the Honey of Life?"

Tellwell Talent
www.tellwell.ca

ISBN
978-0-2288-0533-5 (Paperback)
978-0-2288-0534-2 (eBook)

This book is dedicated in loving memory of my mother
Thérèse Gervais
A pioneering woman who dedicated
her life in service to others

Contents

Preface

This work is presented for information purposes and is not meant to be used as a guide for diagnosing and/ or treating medical and psychological/mental issues. In those instances where medical assistance may be required, it is recommended to seek advice and treatment from a qualified, licensed physician.

In my previous book <u>Spiritual Portraits of the Energy Release Points - A Compendium of Acupuncture Point Messages Found Within the 12 Meridians and 8 Extraordinary Vessels</u>, the idea was presented that the body communicates messages that are held deeply within the physical consciousness. Messages that are heard and activated through the conscious connection to the Energy Release Points.

WHAT ARE ENERGY RELEASE POINTS?

Energy Release Points are little vortexes of energy that are part of the Energy Release Channels. The movement of the Energy Release Points is subtle, however, address profound imbalances which occur on the physical, emotional, mental and spiritual levels. The purpose of Energy Release Points is to release energy as well as bring new energy in. Each Energy Release Point has a specific, deeper meaning which is connected to the physical, emotional, mental and spiritual aspects of the body. These

Energy Release Points are constantly flowing energy through the movement of the vortex, however, sometimes because of life experiences, these Points may become blocked or constricted in their ability to flow energy. This constriction causes an imbalance (disharmony) to show up in one or more of our body systems. These imbalances can be re-harmonized by using mind/heart consciousness to connect with the spirit of the energy in the point. This re-harmonization is followed by exploring and understanding the reason behind the imbalance and then asking it to unblock and activate. Understanding the issue and the message of the spirit of the Energy Release Point is key to personal self healing and empowerment. These Energy Release Points can also be further treated physically should one choose to explore acupuncture or acupressure healing techniques. Ultimately, the goal is to evolve in our understanding of how we create the imbalances within our energy, in order to re-harmonize the body to health and wellness.

Working with these messages of the Energy Release Points with clients as well as receiving feedback from students and readers, affirmations became the next step. Something tangible that can be said in order to reaffirm the healing process taking place in the body. The creation of each affirmation was achieved during meditation on the message of each individual point. The intention of this book of affirmations is to enhance and broaden the depth of healing as well as provide positivity and joy, in order to manifest a meaningful life.

WHAT ARE AFFIRMATIONS?

Affirmations are positive statements that serve to bridge a physical reality and experience with the activity and consciousness of the higher mind, ultimately linking to the Divine Mind. The expression of an affirmation activates processes within the field of consciousness of the mind which initiate connection with a larger field of soul consciousness. The process of an affirmation therefore orders and harmonizes thought with higher Spiritual Consciousness of the Divine Mind serving to activate and integrate the spiritual, mental, emotional bodies within the physical consciousness. Affirmations therefore have powerful impact in strengthening ones ability to manifest positive change within self which ultimately leads to change within humanity. Effectively raising human/world consciousness.

Affirmations of the Energy Release Points, as described in the book Spiritual Portraits of the Energy Release Points - A Compendium of Acupuncture Point Messages Found Within the 12 Meridians and 8 Extraordinary Vessels, assist the body to make the connections between the spiritual portraits and the encoded potentials of Divinity. These encoded potentials are innately embedded within the physical body. The connection to the Energy Release Point unlocks full potential. Through conscious activation and unblocking imbalances found within the Energy Release Points, layers unfold to harmonize in a deeper internalized way through the addition of an affirmation of a message that the body already knows.

When one works through the messages of the Energy Release Points one activates an awareness. The awareness that you are a magnet, and that which is held within the Essence of your heart and your Being determines the reality you live and express. It is this awareness which leads to healing. If within the essence of the heart there is peace, you will attract peace. If there is violence you will attract violence. Vibrationally speaking vibrations of joy, peace and love are more positive and higher in consciousness than vibrations of anger, violence and greed. What gives these vibrations their power is the emotion behind them. When consciousness chooses to resolve and transform lower vibrations as well as master the emotional charge behind these vibrations, disharmonies in the body and subsequently in the life experience will resolve.

Affirmations serve to reinforce positive emotional/mental charge found in the emotional/mental plane thereby bridging the spiritual plane with the physical plane. They reinforce the conscious awareness from the spiritual portrait of the Energy Release Point and magnetize the higher vibrational frequency. As such, working with affirmations helps one to balance polarity and stay in centre. This provides a powerful tool in healing therapy.

This book is presented in the groupings of the Energy Release Channels. Each chapter will have a description of the inherent energy of the Channel in question. This will be followed with the affirmations for each Energy Release Point.

SOME SUGGESTIONS AS TO
HOW TO USE THIS BOOK

This book can be used in conjunction with my first book <u>Spiritual Portraits of the Energy Release Points-A Compendium of Acupuncture Point Messages Found Within the 12 Meridians and 8 Extraordinary Vessels</u>. Consciously contemplate the message of the point. Read the affirmation. The affirmation is a powerful statement that provides a connecting thought that builds and nourishes the healing. Repeat the affirmation several times, as well as several times throughout the day. A second way to use this book is as a divination tool to intuitively connect to one's inner wisdom. In this way, one can contemplate the affirmation, repeating it several times throughout the day. Thirdly, it can be used on a daily basis by integrating the affirmation as part of a gratitude or prayer practice, or as a seed thought for a meditation practice. Finally, as with my first book, these affirmations can be used in conjunction with acupuncture or acupressure treatments. The patient is encouraged to find the affirmations which correspond to the acupuncture points being treated by the practitioner. In this way, one is empowered to be a proactive participant in one's own healing. It is my desire that you, the reader explore many methods of use, allowing this resource to enrich the process of manifesting health, wholeness and joy.

The Lung

The inherent energy of the Lungs is to receive spirit, the inspirations which regulate the quality of life. It holds the energy of the Divine Masculine which is strongly supported by the Divine Feminine. The Divine Masculine provides the catalyst to spark the fire of transformation while the support of the Divine Feminine holds the energy as seeds filled with potential to nourish the passions of the heart. The Lungs surround the heart and therefore minister to the energy of guidance from the promptings of Spirit as inspired from the Creative Force. This ensures that life is prolific, abundant and inspired, assuring the presence of vitality needed for Soul growth and evolution.

When the Lung is out of harmony there is rigidity, inflexibility and hopelessness.

LU - 1 Central Treasury

I connect to Source and access Highest Wisdom for conscious living.

LU - 2 Cloud Gate

I identify my sources of pain and transform them into wholeness through the light within my heart.

LU - 3 Heavenly Palace

I find within myself the highest expression of Heavenly inspiration.

LU - 4 Valiant White

I raise my consciousness to the purity of Unconditional Love.

LU - 5 Foot Marsh / Ghost Reception / Ghost Hall

I listen to the inner promptings of my True Self and align my actions with intention for the Highest Good of All.

LU - 6 Greatest Hole

I release the illusion of separation and reconnect with the pulse of life.

LU - 7 Broken Sequence

I breathe with the rhythm of life and bring myself to balance and centre.

LU - 8 Energy Release Channel Gutter

I shine the light of my Essential Self as a living example of inspiration, joy and positive manifestation.

LU - 9 Great Abyss / Great Spring / Ghost Heart

I AM the rhythm of Life.

LU - 10 Fish Region

I connect with the alchemy of creation, breaking through stagnation and emotional coldness.

LU - 11 Ghost Truth

I AM a priceless treasure.

The Large Intestine

The inherent energy of the Large Intestine is that of transportation and transformation of the inessential in order to be able to receive the new. It functions in partnership with the lungs and represents the breath of the Universal energy as represented by the 5th universal law which states "The ALL is rhythm". The mucosa and submucosa hold on to emotions and it is necessary to allow emotions to flow. The Large Intestine is also responsible for releasing the energy of limiting belief systems which is a necessity in the creation of a new life.

When the Large Intestine is out of harmony everything is blocked or carelessly released without discernment.

LI - 1 Brilliant Exchange

I integrate my Soul with my physical body through the breath of Spirit.

LI - 2 Between Two, The Second Interval

I embrace opposites, alchemically transforming duality into wholeness.

LI - 3 Small Valley, Third Interval

I create the space to process life events in order to release the inessential and receive a new perspective.

LI - 4 Joining of the Valleys

I choose to release suffering and connect with higher consciousness and vibration.

LI - 5 Stream of Masculine Energy

I connect to my inner light and radiate my gifts from my strong centre of love, balance and harmony.

LI - 6 Side Passage

I allow Divine inspiration to guide me into a place of calm during times of transition and change.

LI - 7 Benevolent Warmth

I explore the depths of my emotional body with gratitude and compassion.

LI - 8 Lower Side

I stand on solid ground and draw support from the stability of the earth.

LI - 9 Upper Integrity

I rise to the highest and best of who I AM and walk my path with unwavering trust in the Divine Plan

LI - 10 Arm Three Measures / Ghost Evil

I flow inspiration into meaningful participation in life.

LI - 11 Crooked Pond / Ghost Minister

I AM open to receive the embrace of both the Divine and Earth Mother consciousness.

LI - 12 Elbow Crevice

I flow with the rhythm of life harmonizing my thinking forces to bring order from chaos.

LI - 13 Arm Five Miles / The Working Strength of Five

I stay in centre and tap into the energy of infinite potential possibilities.

LI - 14 Upper Arm

My True Self acknowledges its inner authority by living its authenticity.

LI - 15 Shoulder Majesty

I extend my Self in heart based service to humanity free from sacrifice.

LI - 16 Great Bone

My empowered Self stands tall as I realize the importance of the gifts I bring to the world.

LI - 17 Heavenly Vessel / Heavenly Summit

I evolve towards Ascension through alignment with my Divine Self, continually striving for enlightenment and illumination.

LI - 18 Support and Rush Out

I release past hurts and am inspired by the freshness of a new vision for a positive and optimistic future.

LI - 19 Grain Hole

I discern the quality of the jewel of truth in my life experiences, release the extraneous and refine my learning.

LI - 20 Welcome Fragrance

I embrace the wholeness, beauty and vibrancy of life.

The Stomach

The inherent energy of the Stomach provides the space to balance and alchemically harmonize the physical, emotional, mental and spiritual bodies as embodied within the central, main and core channels of the energy body. It represents the vitality of nourishment and our perceptions of our experience as presented in all aspects of life. (In past, present, parallel and potential future life). It holds the energy of the Divine Feminine and is supported by the energy of the Divine Masculine, allowing us to follow our path with stability.

When the Stomach is out of harmony there is a disconnection with the Earth, leading to insecurity, instability, confusion and distress.

ST - 1 Receive Tears / Flowing Tears

I flow my emotions, cleansing and understanding my emotional pain.

ST - 2 Energy of Four Whites

I connect to my Soul's perfect memory to realize and express my creative potential.

ST - 3 Great Hole

I connect to the strength and courage of my inner Being, accessing the freedom to live my authentic Self knowing I AM stable and secure.

ST - 4 Earth Granary / Earth Greening

The Earth is an unlimited source of nourishment and abundance and I know that ALL is provided for me NOW.

ST - 5 Great Welcome

I connect to my intrinsic self worth, dignity and self respect open to the greatness of my potential as I receive and welcome life.

ST - 6 Jaw Vehicle / Motion Gate / Ghost Forest

I acknowledge what is essential for giving and receiving, empowered by the healthy expression of my needs.

ST - 7 Lower Passage of Earth

I strengthen my roots into the Essence of Earth connecting to the network of Plenty and I AM empowered in my ability to give and to receive.

ST - 8 Head Tied

I detach from worry and connect to the truth and wisdom of my heart, creating order and harmony in my mind.

ST - 9 Welcoming Humanity as Part of All

I connect to my centre, feel communion and belonging to the Earth and I open to receive and feel my connection with the Universal ALL.

ST - 10 Water Rushing Out / Water Gate / Water Heaven

I harmonize my communication with my heart and speak for what I need from a place of love and emotional balance.

ST - 11 Spirit Cottage

I welcome Spirit into my body and nourish the communication between my mind and heart, finding contentment, stability and peace.

ST - 12 Broken Bowl

I move through grief and loss reconstructing that which is shattered.

ST - 13 Door of Vital Nourishing Energy

I draw on the vitality of life and flow with a flexible open mind.

ST - 14 Storehouse

I unify Divine wisdom and inspiration with the vitality of my physical body and fulfill my potential for my life purpose.

ST - 15 Feather Screened Room

I flow my heartfelt love, beauty and vulnerability allowing for the gentle expression of intimacy.

ST - 16 The Window of the Breast

I re-establish my connection to sacred love, security, stability and comfort from the strength and nurturance of my inner centre.

ST - 17 Centre of the Breasts

I heal the insecurities of my inner child through nurturance of my Self.

ST - 18 Root of the Breasts

I reach into the wholeness of my core and connect to the vitality drawn from my ability to nourish Self so that I may nurture others.

ST - 19 Not at Ease

I surrender to the serenity of acceptance, trusting in the Divine Plan and perfect resolutions.

ST - 20 Receive and Support Fullness

I feel my connection to my inner abundance and express my generosity knowing that I continually receive the support and generosity of the Divine.

ST - 21 A Bridging Gateway

I view and digest life from an elevated perspective feeling centred in calm and tranquility.

ST - 22 Illuminated Gate / Gate of Light

I open the gate of clarity and transform my life experiences into illuminated wisdom empowering the manifestation of my highest potential.

ST - 23 Supreme Unity

I strengthen my integrity and alignment to Soul's purpose and follow through with my intentions to manifest my Divine potential.

ST - 24 Lubricating Gateway

I slow down and flow with the pace of life, finding calm within the chaos.

ST - 25 Celestial Pivot

I ground into the Earth, gracefully navigating life with anchored stability.

ST - 26 Outer Mound to Understanding

I connect to the heart of wisdom, strengthening my awareness and understanding of my sacred destiny.

ST - 27 The Great Elder

My growth and evolution are strengthened and supported through accessing my constitutional vitality and flowing it through my body.

ST - 28 Water Path

I follow The Way, flowing myself back to the Source.

ST - 29 The Return

I pause and reflect on events of my past and receive the flow of wisdom from my Soul Essence in order to heal and move forward in life.

ST - 30 Rushing Energy / Thoroughfare of Energy

I consciously flow energy from my mind to my heart and connect to my will, choosing an empowered life.

ST - 31 Network of Strength / Thigh Gate

I put my ideas and visions into action, embracing my life with flexibility and joy as I step into living my ideas and visions.

ST - 32 Crouching Hare

I manifest decisive action while honouring the physical vitality and integrity of my body.

ST - 33 Market of the Mysterious Feminine

Through ritual and ceremony I honour the creative process of my inner divinity.

ST - 34 Beam Mound

I find tranquility and calm within the circle of mindfulness.

ST - 35 Calf's Nose

I face my responsibilities with healthy enthusiasm and joy, knowing that I AM supported and loved.

ST - 36 Leg Three Miles / Lower Tomb / Ghost Evil

I AM grounded, centred and stable.

ST - 37 Upper Great Void / Upper Purity

I experience eternal freedom in the Light through my connection and inspiration of God Force energy.

ST - 38 Lines Opening

I find calm and tranquility within the release of the inessential.

ST - 39 Lower Great Void

I AM in unity with ALL that is and find joy in my process of my journey.

ST - 40 Abundant Splendour

I acknowledge my self worth, see the gifts of my authentic Self and unlock the energy of motivation to manifest my potential.

ST - 41 Stream of Release

I re-establish the flow of inspiration and participation in life through the healing and releasing of the pain of my past.

ST - 42 Meet and Surrender

I find strength through the act of surrender.

ST - 43 Sinking Valley

I find centre and balance through acts of self nurturance, honouring alignment to my Divine Self for meaningful presence on Earth as a bearer of light.

ST - 44 Inner Courtyard

I connect my mind to calm and experience tranquility.

ST - 45 Hard Bargain

I AM flexible within my ability to give and to receive.

The Spleen

The inherent energy of the Spleen is that of storage and distribution of vitality through a complex transportation system bringing nourishment throughout the body via the circulatory and lymphatic systems. This nourishment has strong vital energy which can penetrate every cell, giving the body its ability to move. Its purposeful question is "How may I serve?". It works in direct partnership with the Stomach, adding the qualities of humility, balance, security and stability.

When the Spleen is out of harmony there is exhaustion, fatigue, struggle and depletion in the full body systems.

SP - 1 Hidden White / Ghost Eye

I embrace my sacredness, empower my freedom and open up to receive nourishment from life.

SP - 2 Great Metropolis

Heartfelt exchanges through loving connections with friends, family and creative pursuits allow my life to flow with fulfillment, contentment and joy.

SP - 3 Supreme White / Venus

I express life from a centre of love, respect, honour and nurturance of my Self, for others and for the Earth.

SP - 4 Yellow Emperor / Grandparent-Grandchild

Prosperity, stability and abundance are my divine birthright and I AM open to create and share for the benefit of humanity.

SP - 5 Merchant Mound

I discern truths from untruths, make choices and release the non-essentials.

SP - 6 Union of the Three Feminine Mysteries

I grow through my creative expression, integrating inspiration, vitality and passion for my manifestation of potential.

SP - 7 Leaking Valley

I move forward in sharing my gifts and talents in joyful service to others.

SP - 8 Earth Motivator

I approach life in a way that nourishes my Soul, knowing when to extend and nurture others and when to receive nourishment in return.

SP - 9 Feminine Spring Mound

I connect to the Source Spring of energy, vitality and renewal.

SP - 10 Sea of Blood / Hundred Insect Nest

I strengthen my vitality and flow my creativity.

SP - 11 Winnower Basket Gate

I access my stores of energy and strengthen my vitality, replenishing my dedication of service to humanity.

SP - 12 Rushing Gate / Palace of Motherly Compassion / Palace of Charity

I protect my vitality from overuse and depletion as I live my service.

SP - 13 Official Residence, Our Home

In my centre of stability and wellbeing, I find the nurturance and strength to manifest my purpose.

SP - 14 Abdomen Knot

I fully embrace life knowing that I am safe and secure.

SP - 15 Great Horizontal

I strengthen my vitality through the release of grief, empowered by my trust in Divine support.

SP - 16 Abdomen Sorrow and Lament

My tears serve to express and heal my sorrow, I AM peace and calm.

SP - 17 Food Drain / Destiny Pass

I ensure the health and strength of my body temple through the sacred art of gathering, preparing and eating my food.

SP - 18 Heavenly Stream

I connect to my sacred Essence and flow my compassion embodying peace and healing light.

SP - 19 Chest Village

I live within the true home of my heart and walk joyfully through life.

SP - 20 Encircling Glory

I flourish with wholeness in response to my devotion to the Divine and my acts of service.

SP - 21 Great Enveloping

I allow myself to feel loved and nurtured through my acts of self care.

The Heart

The inherent energy of the Heart is that of our 'I AM Presence" and therefore our inner divinity. It is foundational to Being and needs to remain open in order to receive loving wisdom from our Essence as connected to the Creative Force. It embodies wisdom, peace and calmness. It is the embodiment of love, and through love can circulate Divine energy throughout all the Energy Release Channels so that the body works harmoniously to exude the energy of peace, joy, compassion, radiance and revitalization.

When the heart is out of harmony, it shows as excessive laughter and false emotionality as well as disturbances of the mind.

HT - 1 Utmost Source / To Reach ALL

I align my heart with the Heart of the Divine Source.

HT - 2 Blue-Green Vibrancy of Spirit

I fully embody my I AM Presence and generate transformative power and growth to consciously create my life.

HT - 3 Little Inner Sea / Lesser Sea

I create the space and circumstances to bring the fruition of all my desires.

HT - 4 Path of Spirit

I connect my heart and Essence and follow my path, finding peace, joy and ONE-ness along the way.

HT - 5 Penetrating the Interior / Return to Home

I integrate my mind with spirit and return to wholeness through conscious awareness of the meaning of my life.

HT - 6 Communication Pass / Stone Palace / Penetrating Gate

I penetrate and make conscious my unconscious stuck emotions allowing access to my authentic Being.

HT - 7 Spirit Gate / Spirit Door / Soul Gate

I connect with the intentions of my Soul within the passageway of my heart.

HT - 8 Inner Treasures of the Lesser Palace

I AM one with the space of tranquility.

HT - 9 Little Thoroughfare

I align my actions with the directives of my heart.

The Small Intestine

The inherent energy of the Small Intestine is the energy of discernment and sorting. It clearly can ascertain what is beneficial and what is not. It can sort in order to keep what is optimum and release all that is extraneous. It can be likened to a well organized office manager and sometimes it is referred to as the brain of the physical body. However, it is the use of alchemy that helps in the transformation and sorting process. Nourishing energy is sent to the heart for circulation to the body, extraneous and non-beneficial elements (both physical and non physical) are sent to the Large Intestine for elimination.

A Small Intestine that is out of harmony cannot connect with clarity and loses the ability to discern or discriminate.

SI - 1 Little Marsh / Little Happiness

My life is balanced and flowing within organized structure.

SI - 2 Forward Valley

I allow light into my depths, opening to receive my heart messages through the exploration of my shadow.

SI - 3 Back Ravine

I navigate through life with flexibility, trusting in the Divine Plan.

SI - 4 Wrist Bone

I extend myself to be of service to humanity and receive nourishment for my Essence.

SI - 5 Sun Warmed Valley

I elevate my consciousness and receive the light of Divine Will to manifest my spiritualized ego.

SI - 6 Nourishing the Old

My suffering is transformed into blessings of peace and gratitude.

SI - 7 Support Uprightness

I know the world by living through my heart.

SI - 8 Small Sea

I consciously release and heal my pain so that I can fully participate in life.

SI - 9 Upright Shoulder / Shoulder Integrity / True Shoulder

I stand in my truth and align with right action.

SI - 10 Shoulder Blade

I stay in balance, flow my energy and nourish the health of my body.

SI - 11 Celestial Gathering / Heavenly Assembly of the Ancestors

I AM one with the wholeness of the ALL.

SI - 12 Grasping the Wind

I remain calm within the chaos, focusing on my purpose.

SI - 13 Crooked Wall

I re-align with my purpose and the integrity of my Higher Self.

SI - 14 Outside the Shoulder

I evaluate my boundaries, exploring my relationship with service versus sacrifice.

SI - 15 Middle of the Shoulder

I stay in conscious awareness of living in balance so that I can see and express my potential.

SI - 16 Window Cage / Window of Heavenly Brightness

I see the beauty and joy of life events through the eyes of gratitude.

SI - 17 Heavenly Appearance

I connect to my Higher Self and shift my perspective.

SI - 18 Cheek Bone Hole / Influential Bone Hole

I inspire others through the expression of my Soul's passion.

SI - 19 Listening Palace

I listen with my spirit and receive pearls of wisdom.

The Urinary Bladder

The Urinary Bladder is the longest Energy Release Channel. It holds a magnificent reservoir of vitality that is capable of nourishing the body with the life force of water. Our physical body is made mostly of water. It is one of the elemental building blocks of life. This is why SOUND is one of the most effective vehicles to heal the body. Sound travels four times more quickly in water than in the air. The energy of the Urinary Bladder is that of endurance, motivation, ambition and determination to see things through, as well as carrying the codes of genetic energy which we can choose to transform. The power of the water element allows for circulation and fluidity of movement.

When the Urinary Bladder is out of harmony we feel lifeless, dry and uncreative. Or we can feel out of control and dispersed.

UB - 1 Eyes Full of Illumination

I open my eyes to the beauty of the present, seeing the radiance of the Creator in ALL.

UB - 2 The Grasping of Bamboo / Origin Pillar

I connect with Ultimate Truth and my core integrity living a fully present life.

UB - 3 Eyebrows Rushing

I actively participate in life with flexibility, vitality and enthusiasm.

UB - 4 Deviating Servant

I transform knowledge into wisdom and master the intentions of my Soul.

UB - 5 Fifth Place

I honour the spiritual laws of balance and my spirit awakens to transformative change.

UB - 6 Receive Light

I accept my responsibility to the realization of my potential for benevolent service to humanity.

UB - 7 Penetrate Heaven / Celestial Connection / Old as the Heavens

I penetrate through the chaos and connect to higher consciousness and become the embodiment of peace.

UB - 8 Connecting Cleft

I allow the flow of Light into every aspect of Being.

UB - 9 Jade Pillow

I raise my consciousness to the Divine, allowing for the release of stress and the reception of grace.

UB - 10 Heavenly Pillar

I connect to my inner pillar of strength aligning myself to heart's wisdom and feel my strength to transcend fear.

UB - 11 Great Shuttle / One Hundred Labours

I re-vitalize my physical body by honouring the rhythmic cycles of nature which flow through life.

UB - 12 Gateway of the Winds

I access flowing vitality to navigate movement towards and through change.

UB - 13 Lung Connection

I inspire Soul filled artistry and manifest my creative potential.

UB - 14 Tower Gate

I stand tall and empowered within the dignity and honour of my boundaries.

UB - 15 Connecting Space of the Heart and Mind

My actions of service align with my integrity, my truth and my heart, thereby anchoring joy and love within my Being.

UB - 16 Tower of the Divine Masculine Director / Tower Benefit / Tower Cover

I respect and support the creation of my energetic interface as it functions to integrate my whole body system for my health and wellbeing.

UB - 17 Diaphragm Connection

I open my heart to embrace higher consciousness.

UB - 18 Ninth Burning Space / Liver Connection

My visions flow into manifestation from a place of contentment and inner tranquility.

UB - 19 Gallbladder Connection

I transform my dreams into reality through accessing my courage for action.

UB - 20 Eleventh Burning Space / Spleen Connection

I realize my Divinity.

UB - 21 Stomach Connection

I integrate my life experiences into a meaning-ful whole.

UB - 22 Energy Transfer to the Three Elixir Fields

I align with my integrity and live balanced harmony.

UB - 23 Essence Palace / Tower Cover

I allow the flow of Creator Life Source Energy to energize my body and ignite my creative process.

UB - 24 Sea of Energy

I connect to the energy of power within my depths and rebuild my vitality.

UB - 25 Large Intestine Connection

I flow with life.

UB - 26 Primordial Gate Connection

I draw vitality from Source and resurrect my strength of purpose.

UB - 27 Small Intestine Connection

I distinguish the good in my life and flow my joy, fuelling vitality for living.

UB - 28 Bladder Connection

I am present and receptive to the unfolding moment.

UB - 29 Central Backbone Strength

I stand up for my Self, my beliefs and my truth.

UB - 30 White Jade Ring

I have the courage to see myself in the full truth of sacredness.

UB - 31 Upper Foramen / Upper Bone Hole / Upper Hole

I nourish my vitality by actively flowing my life path with clarity and strength of purpose.

UB - 32 Second Sacral Opening

I open the passage to wisdom and receive illumination.

UB - 33 Centre of the Sacral Bone

I honour and respect my physical body as a temple for my Sacred Self.

UB - 34 Lower Sacral Bone

I ground my higher wisdom of my Soul into the earth, living my wholeness in unity with ALL.

UB - 35 Gathering of Masculine Strength and Vitality

I shift my little will to Divine Will and embrace my Spiritualized Ego.

UB - 36 Attached Branch

I belong.

UB - 37 Door of the Corporeal Soul

I let go of non-serving attachments and connect with my true spiritual ego.

UB - 38 Connection to the Richness of the Vital Region

I have courage to shine light within my darkness, healing and releasing my karma.

UB - 39 Soul Hall

I realize the sacredness of my Being.

UB - 40 Wail of Grief

I move through intense emotions with inner stability.

UB - 41 Diaphragm Border

I release my emotions allowing my physical/spiritual body to harmonize with calm.

UB - 42 Gate of the Ethereal Soul

I connect to the vision of my Soul and realize my oneness with humanity, living and contributing my highest integrity.

UB - 43 Net of Masculine Essentials of Energy

I manifest the vision of my Soul through living the plan of my life with flowing vitality.

UB - 44 Dwelling Place of Thought

I harmonize and refine my thoughts with higher consciousness, creating intentional action for service in the world.

UB - 45 Stomach Granary of Gold

I accept my Soul's invitation to experience all aspects of life.

UB - 46 Gate of Energy to the Vital Centres

I open the gate to my etheric interface and activate my body's ability to self heal and regenerate through the circulation of light.

UB - 47 Chamber of Will / Room of Potential

I activate my desire and determination to realize my potential.

UB - 48 Vital Centre of Womb and Heart

I connect and integrate my heart energy with the vitality of my creative energy.

UB - 49 The Sequence of Orderly Boundaries

I strengthen healthy boundaries of self care in order to develop my gifts for beneficial contribution to the world.

UB - 50 Receive Support

I allow myself to receive support.

UB - 51 Gate of Abundance

I flow energy and fulfill the desires of my heart, manifesting my abundance and living my joy.

UB - 52 Floating Reserves of Energy

I AM joy within my heart.

UB - 53 Balance of Masculine Energy

I restore the balance of energy found within the centre of chaos, accessing my inner stillness.

UB - 54 Central Equilibrium

I take decisive action from my centre of stability.

UB - 55 Unified Forces

I AM filled with Sun Source Vitality and actively manifest my potential in the world.

UB - 56 Supporting Muscles

I AM always supported by the Divine.

UB - 57 Supporting Mountain

I AM support, strength, stability and balance.

UB - 58 Take Flight and Scatter

I AM calm and steady in the face of fear and chaos.

UB - 59 To Access Masculine Energy

I maintain strong energy to release toxic stagnations from my whole physical/spiritual system.

UB - 60 Kunlun Mountain

I transform fear into wisdom, activating my desire and passion for re-birth.

UB - 61 Servant's Aid / Quieting of Evil

I break free of limitations, courageously following my path and destiny.

UB - 62 Extended Vessel / Ghost Road

I receive and access Universal Truths, transforming wisdom into empowerment for self fulfillment and for service to others.

UB - 63 Golden Gate / Bridge Pass

I AM safe.

UB - 64 Capital Bone / Central Bone

I circulate my energy throughout my whole physical/ spiritual system, creating health and wellness for my life journey.

UB - 65 Bone Binder / Thorn Bone

I AM a living wholeness of flowering potential.

UB - 66 Penetrating Valley

Serenity is my natural state of Being.

UB - 67 Extremity of the Divine Feminine Matrix

I connect to the preciousness of my sacredness and realize my potential.

The Kidney

The Kidney works in partnership with the Urinary Bladder. The energy of the Kidneys is similar to the role of a wise and honoured teacher. The Kidneys empower the movement of water and hold the keys to genetic memories. From here stems will, purpose, vitality, strength and creativity. The ability to connect to the wisdom of the jewels of past experiences, heal relationships and imbalances learned through the genetic lineage form the energetics of the Kidney.

When the Kidney is out of harmony there is fear, feelings of being unrooted, lack of vitality, strength and creativity.

KID - 1 Bubbling Spring / Burst of Vibrancy

I rejuvenate and replenish my whole body systems through my connection with the Great Source of All Life.

KID - 2 Blazing Valley / Dragon in the Abyss

I AM magnificence and strength, the embodiment of creativity and transformational magic.

KID - 3 Great Mountain Stream

I connect to and integrate vitality of the great Source of ALL and am nourished by its active living water.

KID - 4 Great Bell

I answer the call of my Soul and fulfill my destiny.

KID - 5 Water Spring

I flow my potential into the world.

KID - 6 Sea of Reflection and Illumination

I AM the embodiment of consciousness, the BE-ing and the DO-ing.

KID - 7 Returning and Repeating Current / Beyond Destiny

I flow with the rhythms and cycles of life.

KID - 8 Sincerity and Trust

I have confidence and trust that my expressions of truth flow freely and are well received by others.

KID - 9 Building Guest

I flow my awakened creativity and birth my potential.

KID - 10 Valley of the Divine Feminine

I flow my life's purpose into the world.

KID - 11 Horizontal Bone / Curved Valley

I AM connected to the deep core of my essence and I honour my sacred wholeness.

KID - 12 Great Glorious Brightness

I unwrap my heart to receive and share the depths of love and authenticity.

KID - 13 Door of Infants

I explore and live a purposeful life through the initiative and manifestation of my free will.

KID - 14 Fullness of Four

I AM moved by the joy of spirit to embrace doing, living and Being.

KID - 15 Central Flow

I actively co-create in the unfoldment of my life through the alignment with my Divine Blueprint.

KID - 16 Vital Centre

I explore and heal my relationship with the Divine Feminine.

KID - 17 Accommodate, Deliberate and Trade / Accommodating Merchant

I assess the value of my gifts and the quality of my expression, allowing for flexibility within my life journey.

KID - 18 Stone Borders / Stone Gate

I open to THE source of nourishment building a strong foundation to digest the experience of life.

KID - 19 Free Passage Within the Inner Capital

I enter the passageway to peace and tranquility.

KID - 20 Through the Valley

I embrace the love and support of the Spiritual Realm, transcending darkness as I emerge into the light.

KID - 21 The Dark Hidden Secret Gate

I allow illumination into my depths of pain transforming fear into wisdom and joy.

KID - 22 Walking on the Verandah

I devote myself to a purposeful life and realize true joy.

KID - 23 Soul Seal of Spirit

I connect to and understand my absolute sacredness of Being.

KID - 24 Spirit Wasteland / Spirit Burial Ground / Spirit Hall

I activate my power and manifest positive change in the world.

KID - 25 Spirit Storehouse

I AM the resonance of my I AM Presence.

KID - 26 Within the Centre of Elegance

I embrace the Light, living and radiating the virtues of my Sacred Self.

KID - 27 Treasury of Source

My actions unfold from my source of infinite vitality.

The Pericardium

The inherent energy of the Pericardium is that of creating a sacred circle around the heart. The circle serves to protect the divinity within one's Being. Representatives of this circle: the virtues of trust, wisdom, generosity, compassion, understanding and love, are responsible for carrying out desires and passions. These appropriate actions manifest the vibrations of joy, calm and radiance of Light within the cellular structure of one's Being.

A pericardium out of harmony cannot trust, is narcissistic, dispassionate and misunderstands the intentions of others.

P - 1 Heavenly Pond

I bathe in the purity of the Holy Spirit, healing my shadows and scars from life.

P - 2 Heavenly Spring / Heavenly Warmth / Heaven's Revival

I embrace life flowing strength and compassion from my healed heart.

P - 3 Crooked Marsh

I set healthy and appropriate boundaries in my intimate relationships.

P - 4 Gate of Energy Reserves

I transform emotional pain of past betrayals creating peace and serenity in my heart, mind and soul.

P - 5 The Intermediary / Ghost Road

My heart exchanges pain and attachments for love and gratitude.

P - 6 Inner Frontier Gate / Inner Palace Gate

I willingly explore pain and hurt in order to transform experiences into blessings of peace.

P - 7 Great Tomb / Ghost Heart

I consciously connect to the sacredness of life and the gifts I bring to the world.

P - 8 Palace of Weariness / Ghost Road

I nourish my light found within the inner chambers of my heart, opening myself to live in fulfillment and joy.

P - 9 Rushing Into the Middle

I seize the day focusing on my vision and living actions for my highest good.

The Three Elixir Fields

The inherent energy of the Three Elixir Fields is that of being the mediator and harmonizing the body in wholeness for it to function at optimum efficiency. This Energy Release Channel connects to the Environmental Part of our energy fields and regulates the inner and outer conditions of life. This regulation is essential in order to live in harmony and balance with what is and with what comes.

When the Three Elixir Fields are out of harmony, we become polarized. Physically this can present as being too hot and too cold at the same time in different parts of the body. On the emotional/mental/spiritual levels this can manifest as conflict.

TH - 1 Rushing the Frontier Gate

I extend my Authentic Self into the world, creating positive interaction within healthy boundaries.

TH - 2 The Gateway of Outer Harmony

I support my True Self through discernment and clarity, harmonizing my inner and outer world.

TH - 3 Middle Islet

I bring my Being to centre empowering my body's ability to self heal.

TH - 4 Pond Source/ Source of Communications / Communications Network

I harmonize the microcosm within me with the macrocosm of the God force knowing I AM ONE with the ALL.

TH - 5 Outer Frontier Gate

I harmonize my inner life with my outer life through my direct connection to my truth.

TH - 6 Flying Tiger / Branched Ditch

I sustain my vitality through the modulation of my energy.

TH - 7 Assembly of Ancestors

I bring conscious awareness and alignment to the jewels of ancestral wisdom, strengthening my foundation to realize my potential and destiny.

TH - 8 Connecting the Interval / Communication Pass / Communication Gate

I communicate with sincerity for co-operative manifestation.

TH - 9 Four Rivers

I flow in flexible direction in all aspects of Being.

TH - 10 Heavenly Well

I embrace balanced living.

TH - 11 Pure Cold Abyss

I flow light throughout my body, warming my heart to compassion and love.

TH - 12 Melting Into Relaxation of Joyful Happiness

I see the beauty around me, relaxing into wellbeing and serenity.

TH - 13 Shoulder / Upper Arm Convergence

I respond to the demands of life in a balanced and flexible way.

TH - 14 Shoulder Bone

I express joyful service from the strength of my alignment to purpose.

TH - 15 Heavenly Crevice / Heavenly Healing

I extend my heart to the world.

TH - 16 Heavenly Window

I know and express my authenticity and truth.

TH - 17 Screen of Wind

I work through change and transformation free from fear.

TH - 18 Regulate and Support the Body

I create the space to nurture harmony, balance and calm.

TH - 19 Skull Breathing

I understand and apply the wisdom learned from my experiences.

TH - 20 Angle Grandchild

I AM the connecting link bridging and bringing wisdom of my ancestors into the present for the future generations.

TH - 21 Gateway of Listening

I listen with the wisdom of my heart, honouring the development of my truth.

TH - 22 Harmony Hollow

I listen with a peaceful mind aligning to life with clear perception.

TH - 23 Silk Bamboo Hollow

I strengthen my wholeness with flexibility and calm, empowering resilience, balance and harmony.

The Gallbladder

The inherent energy of the Gallbladder is that of the embodiment of courage in the flesh. It means bravery, courage and the ability to make decisions, give direction of these decisions into precise goals and to purposefully follow through with positive action. The energy also embodies discernment, integrity and justice. Positive action with strength, flexibility, grounded enthusiasm and optimism. It is an overcomer of obstacles.

When the Gallbladder is out of harmony we have conflict, indecision and the feelings of irritation.

GB - 1 The Sun, Before the Pass

The Light guides and supports me as I move through passages of darkness, bringing me to my natural state of harmony with life.

GB - 2 Hearing Laughter after the Pass

I trust in the process of life, maintaining the experience of joy.

GB - 3 Above the Pass / Guest Host Man/ Easy Host/ The Great Sun

I AM the embodiment of Love, my heart and hands open to flow sharing and receiving.

GB - 4 Loathsome Jaws / Fullness of the Head

I AM inner tranquility transforming inner conflicts through clear expression.

GB - 5 Suspended Skull

I integrate Divine inspiration with the wisdom of my heart, unblocking my potential for expansion through clarity of action.

GB - 6 Suspended Tuft / Suspended Hair

I realize the blessings of grace and find contentment within simplicity.

GB - 7 The Maze of the Temples

I connect to my inner centre and navigate the journey of life with the intuitive wisdom of my I AM presence.

GB - 8 Flowing Valley

I follow the directives of my vision and purpose, opening to receive the riches around me.

GB - 9 Celestial Hub / Celestial Crossroads

I align with Cosmic vision and have clarity for purposeful action.

GB - 10 Floating Pure White Energy

I AM connected to my true authentic self through simplicity of Being.

GB - 11 Receptivity Within the Feminine Space of the Mind

I listen and receive higher guidance and flow my words for clear manifestation of my desires.

GB - 12 Final Bone / Completion

I allow myself the space to rest and contemplate my journey.

GB - 13 Root Spirit

I anchor my Soul vision into my physical body, grounding my clarity and focus for conscious manifestation.

GB - 14 Pure and Clear Masculine Energy

I embrace the day of endless possibilities flowing from moment to moment.

GB - 15 Head Directed by the Kindness of Tears

I allow the flow of healing tears to release the pain of the past, moving me forward in alignment with right action of my True Self.

GB - 16 Windows of the Eyes / Arriving to Greatest Glory

I raise my consciousness to the wisdom of experience, creating a higher perspective in service to the evolution of my Soul.

GB - 17 Upright Living

I nourish the vision of my Soul essence through my alignment to living the right action of my authentic Self.

GB - 18 Receiving Spirit

I AM conscious of who I AM.

GB - 19 Vastness of the Brain

I allow freedom of thought and receive illumination.

GB - 20 Wind Pond

I connect to and receive clarity from my awakened consciousness to implement positive action during the process of change and chaos.

GB - 21 Shoulder Well

I honour the needs of my Self and transform servitude into joyous service.

GB - 22 Humour Gate

Laughter and balanced living bring me health and vitality.

GB - 23 Attached Tendon / Spirit Light

I stand upright connected to my path, navigating life with ease and freedom.

GB - 24 Sun and Moon the Great Illuminators

I perceive the world of opposites and strengthen my ability to balance my awareness of reality.

GB - 25 Capital Gate

I access the wealth of my Soul Essence for conscious creation and expression of my perfect work, embracing the energy of fulfilled desire, abundance and freedom.

GB - 26 Girdling Vessel of Vital Circulation

My Soul embraces the magnificence of living in the world through the sensory experiences of my physical body.

GB - 27 Fifth Pivot

I anchor my strength and stay in balance remaining flexible in action towards the fulfillment and manifestation of my creativity.

GB - 28 Maintain the Way

I maintain my commitment to walking my life path, trusting my ability to navigate the unknown.

GB - 29 Dwelling in the Strength of the Bone

I have the strength and courage to follow my own path.

GB - 30 Jumping Circle

I joyously spring into action with clear intention of my centred Self.

GB - 31 Market of the Winds

I navigate changes with flexibility and grace, flowing with the rhythm of life.

GB - 32 Middle of the Ditch

I stand in centre and observe the opposites of life realizing the wholeness and unity within the ALL.

GB - 33 Passageway of Masculine Forces

I AM strong, flexible and adaptable within my plans and goals.

GB - 34 Masculine Spring Mound

I participate in life open to new points of view and higher perspectives, nurturing the learning and growth of my Soul.

GB - 35 Masculine Intersection

I harness my powerful masculine energy for action and the completion of goals.

GB - 36 Outer Mound

I contemplate my unlimited potential as I view the vibrant panorama of my life horizon.

GB - 37 Bright, Clear Illumination

I consciously connect my Soul vision with the Divine Light of Illumination and begin the action towards positive manifestation.

GB - 38 Supported by the Strength of Masculine Power

The spark of my heart is awakened, renewing my passion to open and flourish with life.

GB - 39 Hanging Cup / Hanging Bell

I AM pure expression, the potential of all Creation.

GB - 40 Wilderness Mound of Ruins

I realize my potential and make change in the world.

GB - 41 Near to Tears

I acknowledge and transform frustration through the release of tears, reconnecting to purposeful action and fulfillment of my life plan.

GB - 42 Earth Five

I connect to my Soul's vision within the flames of my heart and stride confidently towards mastery of my purpose.

GB - 43 Valiant Stream

With courage and perseverance, I flow in the process of Soul growth, discerning service from servitude.

GB - 44 To Walk From a Place of Inner Light and Stillness

I value the uniqueness of my Essence and embrace the nature of my Being.

The Liver

The inherent energy of the Liver is the energy of the Soul's vision and purpose. It is the energy of the Master planner - the Supreme All Knowing. It is through the liver that we can connect to the master blueprint of life direction, refining our Essence to become who we are meant to be, regardless of whatever circumstances are brought to us.

When the Liver is out of harmony, we over-plan or do not plan. We can feel hopeless and often experience anger. The anger, however, can be positive, showing us that something needs to change.

LIV - 1 Wellspring of Esteem and Sincerity

I align my integrity with my inner vision and my life flows.

LIV - 2 To Walk Between

I flow in harmony and balance as I transform inspiration into positive action.

LIV - 3 Great Forging of Happy Calm

I fully embrace all that life brings, seeing the jewel in all my experiences.

LIV - 4 Middle Seal

I bring my Life Plan into action through my connection and alignment with my Sacred Essence.

LIV - 5 Insect Drain

I AM empowered by the action of purification, restoring my vision and my understanding of my Soul Plan.

LIV - 6 The Metropolis / The Moon

I AM vitality and regeneration.

LIV - 7 The Flexible Network / Knee Pivot

I AM unlimited potential.

LIV - 8 Crooked Spring

I flow around obstacles with flexibility staying focused on my goals.

LIV - 9 Envelope of the Inner Feminine

I AM sacred wholeness.

LIV - 10 Five Miles

I AM freedom.

LIV - 11 The Feminine Angle of Modesty

I see the beauty of who I AM and I emerge from the darkness into the light.

LIV - 12 Urgent Stirred Vessel / Goat Arrow

I AM vital creative energy.

LIV - 13 Chapter Gate / Completion Gate

I step forward towards new life experiences.

LIV - 14 Gate of Hope / Expectation's Door

I AM fully in the NOW, trusting in Divine co-creation of a joy-filled, meaningful life.

The Divine Feminine Matrix
(Conception Vessel)

The Energy Release Channel of the Divine Feminine Matrix is the aspect of the Divine Feminine Energy within the Creative Force which is responsible for co-creation of the physical. It is partnered with the Divine Masculine Energy and work together for creation. It travels in a clockwise energetic pattern of direction. It is, however, responsible for the germination and potential of all existence. It is the vessel through which all life comes. (Although it is the energy of the Divine Masculine that activates and pushes life forward) It is within this matrix that the Creative Force encodes purpose, and it is this connection to purpose that gives Life meaning. The Divine Feminine Matrix is the energy that creates and governs our vital resources, as connected to Soul, through the creation of our etheric and whole body systems. Connection with this Energy Release Channel allows for access to the inner nourishment that is necessary to develop our service along the life path. This Energy Release Channel provides harmony and balance and it alchemically transforms inspiration into creation. It is about the fertility of life.

When the Divine Feminine Matrix is out of balance there can be feelings of being ungrounded, shaky, or fragile; inability to create new ideas; inability to make plans and set goals; fear causing stagnation; apprehension or avoidance of threshold experiences; low self esteem; fear of sexual intimacy; lack of self love. Physical manifestation of night sweating; hot flashes; mental irritability; anxiety; dry mouth at night; dizziness; tinnitus; insomnia; chronic asthma.

DFM - 1 Meeting of the Inner Seas / The Golden Door / Ghost Store

My vitality and strength are restored through the alchemical union of spirit, soul and body.

DFM - 2 Crooked Bone / Encircling Bone

I connect and explore the deep inner recesses of my Being, transforming pain and darkness through the embracement of my sanctity.

DFM - 3 Central Pole of the Jade Spring

I stay in balance, observing the flow of life as I navigate my journey.

DFM - 4 Gate of the Source

I AM ONE with the womb of creation and life.

DFM - 5 Stone Gate

I connect with the centre of my strength and wisdom, empowered to live fully in the world.

DFM - 6 Sea of Abundantly Flowing Energy

I harmonize with the cycles of nature, restoring my vitality and passion to flow my creative potential.

DFM - 7 Feminine Crossing

I explore and understand the internal consciousness of my Sacred Self.

DFM - 8 Gate of the Watchtower of Spirit

I AM an expression of the mystic miraculous connected to the Source Eternal of Life.

DFM - 9 The Flowing Division of Water

I flow consciousness from the watery depths of Source into all aspects of my Being.

DFM - 10 Dark Gate Into the Core

I open the gate into the depths of my Being and explore the mysteries of my Self.

DFM - 11 Interior Strengthening / To Build Within

I release pain of the past, receive inspiration of the NOW and shift into higher frequencies of harmony.

DFM - 12 Central Core

My emotional centre is stable and balanced within the rhythm of life.

DFM - 13 Upper Heavenly Core

I accept nourishment and nurturing in all aspects of my Being.

DFM - 14 Great Watch Tower

I connect with the passion found within the inner chambers of my heart and joyfully express the gifts I bring to the world.

DFM - 15 Loving Protection of the Dove

I flow the spirit of Peace and Love through the wholeness of my Being.

DFM - 16 Middle Palace Courtyard

I receive the Holy Spirit within the sacred palace of my heart, reclaiming my will to serve the Divine.

DFM - 17 Centre of the Inner Storehouse of Light

I AM the embodiment of love, radiating light in all that I do.

DFM - 18 Jade Hall / Precious Gem

I AM a living expression of my Soul Song, amplifying and radiating the light from within.

DFM - 19 Purple Palace

My physical body expresses the sacred divinity of my Soul.

DFM - 20 Magnificent Floral Canopy

I connect to the birthplace of my Soul and flow the energy of light through the breath of life.

DFM - 21 Jade Within the Pearl

Through the cultivation of wisdom within my treasure of jewels, I realize my potential and devotion to my purpose.

DFM - 22 Celestial Chimney, the Opening of the Heavens

I flow with the Universal breath of Spirit.

DFM - 23 Majesty's Spring

I recognize the brilliance of who I AM, humble yet honoured and blessed to step forward in service to humanity.

DFM - 24 Receiving Fluid

I AM purified and cleansed by the flow of Spirit.

The Divine Masculine Director (Governor Vessel)

The Energy Release Channel of the Divine Masculine Director is the aspect of the Divine Masculine Energy within the Creative Force, which is responsible for co-creation of the physical. It is partnered with the Divine Feminine Energy and work together for creation. If the Divine Feminine generates the potentials, it is the Divine Masculine that puts these potentials into motion. It is the action. It travels in a counter-clockwise energetic pattern of direction. It creates and guides all communication that enables all the energy bodies, in all aspects and all directions, to work together in unified purpose. It is the inner vitality that draws on the resources from the movement of Spirit and its connection to Source. Connection to the Divine Masculine strengthens the energy of Divine Will with the flexibility of Cosmic Love.

When the Divine Masculine Director is out of balance, there can be issues relating to survival and poverty consciousness; inability to flow with life; disconnection to Spirit; over-striving beyond physical limits; fatigue; inner conflict with reconciling the material with Spiritual existence; lack of integrity; inability to act on creative impulses. Physical manifestations of lower back pain; headaches; neurological disorders; poor memory.

DMD - 1 Stairway to Heaven / Long and Strong Thrust of Energy

My vitality renews and reinvigorates my strength to emerge and create.

DMD - 2 Loins Birth

My vitality fuels my passion and desire to focus my energy of creation.

DMD - 3 Border of the Loins

I keep my feminine and masculine energies in balance.

DMD - 4 Gate of Life, Destiny and Purpose

I embrace and flow my passion, power and vitality into manifestation of my purpose.

DMD - 5 Suspended Pivot

My Soul expresses through the flow of spirit.

DMD - 6 Central Pillar

My actions are aligned with my commitment to my divinity and the I AM Presence.

DMD - 7 Balanced Central Pivot

I open to all possibilities and move gracefully through changes with centred balance and vitality.

DMD - 8 Ease and Strength

I balance, integrate and harmonize my masculine power with my feminine nurturing energy.

DMD - 9 To Reach the Utmost High

I transcend the darkness through the vision of heaven, re-aligning with the strength to continue the manifestation of my potential.

DMD - 10 Supernatural Tower / Spirit Tower / Spirit's Platform

I choose connection with the Forces of Light honouring the sacredness of my heart.

DMD - 11 Spirit Path

I hear the whispering of my Soul within the calmness of my mind.

DMD - 12 Sustaining Pillar of Life

I stand erect with truth and integrity, courageously creating a flourishing life.

DMD - 13 Kiln Path / Fires of Transformation

I AM eternal within the ALL.

DMD - 14 Great Hammer / Hundred Taxations

My spiritual body integrates and flows healing grace within my full body systems.

DMD - 15 Gate of Dumbness / Loss of Voice

I AM free to speak, sing and laugh.

DMD - 16 Palace of the Wind / Ghost Forest

I renew my strength and vitality to energize and defend my physical/spiritual system.

DMD - 17 Brain Door / Brain Household / Encompassing Wind

I guide my thoughts, words and actions with the wisdom of my heart.

DMD - 18 Strength Between / Great Feather

I stand in self empowerment acting for the highest good and benefit of ALL.

DMD - 19 Posterior Summit / Behind the Vertex

I harmonize my consciousness with flexibility and receptivity.

DMD - 20 Meeting in Grand Unity / One Hundred Convergences / The One, Three, Five

The ALL is in the ONE and I AM ONE within the ALL.

DMD - 21 Heavenly Anterior Summit

I connect to my Higher Self and raise my consciousness to the wholeness of the ALL.

DMD - 22 Skull Meeting / Ghost Gate

I continue to grow and evolve towards the manifestation of my perfected Being.

DMD - 23 Heavenly Star / Spirit Hall / Ghost Mansion

My inner vision beholds the path of illuminated wisdom and my place within the cosmic tapestry of the Ascension path.

DMD - 24 Sacred Courtyard of the I AM

I see and recognize Divine consciousness within all things.

DMD - 24.5 Hall of Impression / Seal Hall

I see myself as I truly am and radiate the light of my sacred identity.

DMD - 25 The Simplicity of the White Unadorned Bone

I return and contemplate my bare Essential Self.

DMD - 26 Waterways to the Centre of my Being / Ghost Guest Room

I reconnect my essence with the mothering forces of the Earth, accepting nourishment to the core of my Being so I may serve others in peace, harmony and joy.

DMD - 27 Correct Exchange / To Open With Correct Reason and Happiness

My alignment to my truth expresses through intentional use of words and actions.

DMD - 28 Mouth of the River Crossing Into the Sea

I flow within the Wholeness of the ALL.